BABY'S FIRST BOOK
ANIMALS

HIGH CONTRAST
BLACK AND WHITE BABY BOOK

SELENA DALE

COPYRIGHT NOTICE

Copyright © 2017 by Selena Dale

All rights reserved. This book or any portion thereof may not be reproduced or used in any manner whatsoever without the express written permission of the publisher except for the use of brief quotations in a book review.

BOOK TIPS

Snuggle up with the book
Your baby will enjoy the snuggling and hearing your voice. He/she will feel safe and secure with you while looking at the images in the book. This builds your baby's confidence and love of reading.

Talk with your baby while looking at the book
Talk about the pictures in the book. By listening, your child will learn words, ideas, and how language works.

Encourage your baby's coos, growls, and gurgles
They are your baby's way of communicating with you, and are important first steps toward speech. The more your baby practices making sounds, the clearer they will become.

Develop a daily routine with this book
Routines will soothe your baby and let him/her learn to predict what will happen next.

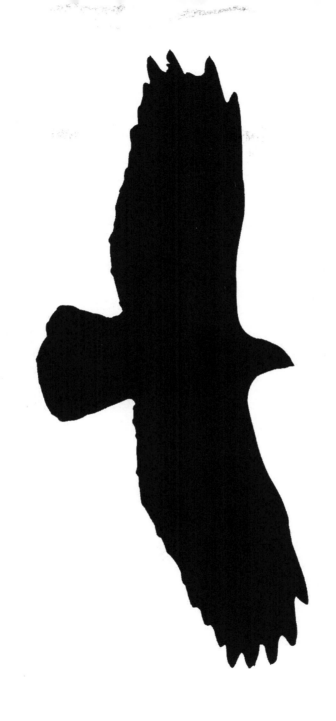

MORE CHILDREN'S BOOKS FROM SELENA DALE

STORY BOOKS, ANIMAL BOOKS, PUZZLE BOOKS AND MORE!

VISIT

amazon.com/author/selenadale

or

www.selenadale.com

Printed in Great Britain
by Amazon